THE MISSION OF GOD

THE GREAT COMMISSION IN ALL OF SCRIPTURE

JOSHUA GILLIAM

ISBN: 9798685922885

DEDICATION

To Joseph Peer, who first helped me see the "all nations" part of the Great Commission.

CONTENTS

ACKNOWLEDGMENTS

The book would not have been possible without the patient instruction of the professors in the Intercultural Studies Department of Columbia International University. I give particular thanks to Dr. Christopher Little. His presentations on the *Missio De* were especially catalytic.

1 INTRODUCTION

For two years I taught tactics to second lieutenants at the Infantry Officer Basic Course in Fort Benning Georgia. One of my jobs was to help each future leader understand how the mission of their platoon fit into the mission of their company and their battalion. For weeks I helped these officers analyze the orders they received from higher-headquarters. They needed to craft their platoon's mission in a way supported and contributed to the larger mission. If their mission did not support the overall mission they would be unnecessary and irrelevant. Often I instructed these lieutenants to "Write it again" as the temptation to *do their own thing* was frequently too great. In myriad ways these men were drilled to ensure their efforts were not singular; they had to be synchronized with – and complementary to – their parent units' mission.

The church today is fractured into a thousand disparate missions. Although we share of common set of scriptures, there are many *rogue platoons*, executing a mission they thought of themselves – a mission that is not synchronized with the mission of the church. On the other side we have leaders who want to sideline these rogue platoons from participating in the mission at all. What the situation requires is education. In the same way that a new platoon leader must be taught to relate their mission with that of their higher-headquarters, Christian leaders must be taught to derive their missions from the mission given us in scripture.

THE GREAT COMMISSION

Christians must clearly understand the overall mission of God before they can relate to it. So, what is the mission God has assigned the church? The commission of Matthew 28:18-20 best answers this question. Allow me to quote this command from the resurrected Christ:

All authority in heaven and on earth has been given to me.[19] Therefore go and make disciples of all nations, baptizing them in the name of the Father and of the Son and of the Holy Spirit,[20] and teaching them to obey everything I have commanded you. And surely I am with you always, to the very end of the age.

This passage is the clearest articulation of God's assigned mission to his people. As the last instruction Jesus gives before his ascension, many churches give Matthew 28 the attention it deserves. However, many other churches miss this passage among a sea of other sayings. And still other sincere followers of Christ believe that Jesus gave his disciples an entirely new command here. Therefore, they place the Great Commission alongside other important sayings of Jesus and thus rob it of its primacy.

But rather than being something new, the great mission of Matthew 28 builds upon a fundamental mission already assigned to God's people with antecedents as far back as Genesis. It originally emerges in the first chapter of Genesis and is developed further during God's dealings with Abraham (Genesis 12). The mission is restated to God's people throughout the Psalms, finding a sharp voice in Psalm 96. The prophets often called Israel back to this mandate, and God often called the prophets back to this mission. Jonah is a great example of God's call to the nations, and we have a full chapter on him.

When it comes to the New Testament, the mission is not only recorded for us in Matthew, but also in Mark, Luke-Acts, and John as well. In these references we will see that even when God's people were slow to respond, God himself is active in driving His mission to it final completion.

It is my aim to establish the Great Commission as God's mission from the very beginning. It is my hope this humble book will excite a zeal in God's people for God's mission. It is my prayer this book will be a catalyst in uniting the church in common purpose. It is my dream – through our collective effort – to stand before him at the end of the age in worship with millions of followers from every tribe, tongue, people, and nation. Let's get started!

2 GENESIS

The first command God gave mankind – indeed the first words God spoke to Adam and Eve – was *"Be fruitful and multiply"* (Genesis 1:22), a few verses later adding, *"fill the earth and subdue it"* (Genesis 1:28). It is interesting that the first thing God told them was to multiply and fill the earth. Of all the things God could have said to his newly-created children, he gave them a global mandate. There seems to be no "Hi, how are you?" or "You are beautiful." Rather, God went right to mission. Fascinating. Indeed, this first command would be the proto-mission that other prophets and apostles – under the inspiration of the Holy Spirit – would develop into what is today the mission of the church. Wenham also sees the command to be fruitful and multiply as proto-typical of ensuring instructions:

This command ... is repeated to Noah after the flood (9:1), and the patriarchs too are reminded of this divine promise (17:2, 20: 28:3; 35:11). The genealogies of Gen 5, 9, 11, 25, 36, 46 bear silent testimony to its fulfillment, and on his deathbed Jacob publicly notes the fulfillment of the divine word (48:4; cf. 47:27).[1]

In contrast, many commentators see these instructions as only pertaining to mans' relationship to animal and plant life, and therefore really only (as the story goes) forming the basis of an environmental mission. As even Matthews says in the conservative *New American Commentary*:

> The mandate to subjugate the world includes the major zoological groups: fish, birds, and land animals. The lists of the animals are only general classifications and vary in details within the account (1:26, 28, 30). This appointment by God gave the human family privilege but also responsibility as "caretakers" (2:15).[2]

Matthews is joined by a host of other voices that culminate in the most recent popular contribution – *The Green Bible: Understand the Bible's Powerful Message for the Earth*.[3]
While some church fathers believed Adam and Eve were commanded to multiply spiritually,[4] most see this passage as pertaining to physical progeny.[5] This is indeed the

---

[1] Gordon J. Wenham, *Genesis 1–15*, vol. 1, *Word Biblical Commentary* (Dallas: Word, Incorporated, 1998), 33.

[2] K. A. Mathews, *Genesis 1-11:26*, vol. 1A, *The New American Commentary* (Nashville: Broadman & Holman Publishers, 1996), 174–175.

[3] *The Green Bible* (New York: HarperCollins, 2008).

[4] Andrew Louth and Marco Conti, eds., *Genesis 1–11*, *Ancient Christian Commentary on Scripture* (Downers Grove, IL: InterVarsity Press, 2001), 38.

[5] Allen P. Ross, "Genesis," in *The Bible Knowledge Commentary: An Exposition of the Scriptures*, ed. J. F. Walvoord and R. B. Zuck, vol. 1 (Wheaton, IL: Victor Books, 1985), 29; Matthew Henry, *Matthew Henry's Commentary on the Whole Bible: Complete and Unabridged in One Volume* (Peabody: Hendrickson, 1994), 6; and Robert Jamieson, A. R. Fausset, and David Brown, *Commentary Critical and Explanatory on the Whole Bible*, vol. 1 (Oak Harbor,

passage's most immediate and literal meaning. However, as this command is echoed through the generations, its volume and scope increases.

In Genesis chapter nine, when Noah's family departs the ark after the flood, God reiterates the marching orders given to Adam:

And God blessed Noah and his sons and said to them, 'Be fruitful and multiply and fill the earth. The fear of you and the dread of you shall be upon every beast of the earth…'

The USB Handbook identifies the word "blessed" in this instance as the same word used in Genesis 1:22 and 1:28.[6] The primary instruction to be fruitful and multiply and fill the earth remains unchanged from God's instructions to Adam. However, this time the animals will be scared of humans. If Adam's original commission pertained to the care of creation, Noah's mandate would then be a complete reversal. Therefore, it is most sensible to view this mandate as having a generational and territorial component but not as a creation-care command. These commands provide the scope of God's mission in respect to land and people – most clearly expressed in Matthew 28 – "*Go into all the world* [mission in respect to land] *and make disciples of all nations*" [mission in respect to people].

This background brings us now to Abram. The instructions given to Abram attach promises to the commands given to Adam and Noah and reveal more precursors to the great commission articulated in Matthew 28. Let's look at the passage:

WA: Logos Research Systems, Inc., 1997), 18.

[6] William David Reyburn and Euan McG. Fry, *A Handbook on Genesis*, UBS Handbook Series (New York: United Bible Societies, 1998), 201.

> *Now the Lord said to Abram, "Go from your country and your kindred and your father's house to the land that I will show you.[2] And I will make of you a great nation, and I will bless you and make your name great, so that you will be a blessing.[3] I will bless those who bless you, and him who dishonors you I will curse, and in you all the families of the earth shall be blessed."* (Gen 12:1:3)

There is only one command in this passage – "Go."[7] Abram was command to go. The imperative is made emphatic by a reflexive pronoun ("Go yourself").[8] Abram was under a divine imperative to "go!" Not only was he commanded to 'go toward', but he was commanded to 'go from' – to leave behind – certain things. God's first and last words to Abram (12:1; 22:1) begin with an imperative to *go*. Both times the command is followed by a triple object: Go from (1) your country, (2) your homeland, and (3) your father's house. In a similar way that Adam's scope was in reference to land and family, Abram was charged with leaving both his land (country, homeland) and his family (father's house). As we shall see, Abram was commanded to leave these things with the promise that God will multiply his family and land in the coming generations. Notice that Abram was commanded to "Go" in much the same way that Jesus commanded his disciples to "Go" in the Great Commission of Matthew 28.[9]

---

[7] Reyburn and McG. Fry, *A Handbook on Genesis*, 272.

[8] K. A. Mathews, *Genesis 11:27–50:26*, vol. 1B, The New American Commentary (Nashville: Broadman & Holman Publishers, 2005), 109.

[9] However, the scribes who translated the Hebrew word "Go" into Greek from the Septuagint, used the verb Ἔξελθε which carries the meaning "to cast out."[9] (whereas the "Go" in Matthew 28 means *travel*).[9] This is the same verb used in Matthew 10:2 for "send" when disciples are told to pray to the Lord of the Harvest to "send." Therefore, these commands are not related by etymology. Nevertheless, they can still be related by theology. Jesus often said things like this about his sent ones:

Starting in verse two God offers Abram some incredible promises. As he obeys the command to "Go" God promises to (1) make him a great nation, (2) bless him and make him great, (3) curse those who dishonor him, and (4) through Abram, bless all the families of the earth. Wow. Abram's obedience to God's mission will affect all the families of the earth. But the term families does not capture the full scope. As William Reyburn writes:

> The Hebrew term is often translated "family" as in RSV. However, its basic meaning is "subdivision," "category," or "clan," and so it generally refers to groups larger than the family group. Speiser translates "All the communities on earth," while REB and NIV have "All [the] peoples on earth," and TEV "All the nations."[10]

Therefore, in Genesis twelve God commands the patriarch to "Go" from his people. And as he obeys all the nations of the earth will be blessed. Notice the relationship to the Great Commission. Like Matthew 28, the scope of God's mission to Abram is all the nations. It was indeed this way from the beginning. Also notice that obedience to God's mission comes with a promise of success. In Genesis 12 it is the promise to bless Abram and through him the nations. In Matthew 28 it is the promise of blessing through His accompanying presence ("I am with you always") that guarantees again the success of the mission – the blessing of the nations.

But there's more. The author of Hebrews says that we are "heirs of the promise" of blessing and multiplication given to Abram (6:14-17). At the popular level, the church

---

("And everyone who has left houses or brother or sisters" [Matthew 19:29]). The present researcher does indeed see theological antecedent to the Great Commission here under the command to go/leave.

[10] Reyburn and McG. Fry, *A Handbook on Genesis*, 275.

today understands that we have Abraham's promise of blessing. But do we understand that we also have Abraham's promise of multiplication? Said plainly, the promise to bless all nations through natural generations (childbirth) is now our inherited promise to bless all nations through spiritual generations (making disciples). It is Matthew 28:20b once again. This same command and promise is reiterated through the whole of Genesis. Take some time to read chapters 18:18; 22:17-18 (Abraham), 26:4 (Isaac), and 28:3 (Jacob).[11] Let us now visit the Psalms.

---

[11] Steven Hawthorne, *"The Story of His Glory" Perspective on the World Christian Movement: A Reader* (Pasadena: William Carey Library, 2009), 49-63.

3 PSALMS 96

In his classic work *A Biblical Theology of Missions,* George Peters said, the "whole psalms are missionary messages and challenges." Study carefully Psalm 2, 33, 66, 72, 98, 117, 145. We could add several more. Space does not permit the exposition of each Psalm listed here. But it's worth noting that the frequency of great commission language in the Psalms is reflective of the scope of the mission. And the emphasis on *all nations* is clear. Here is a small sample:

> *"May God be gracious to us and bless us and make his face to shine upon us that your way may be known on the earth, your saving power among the nations. … Oh let the nations be glad and sing for joy." (67:1,2,4)*

> *"Praise the Lord all nations! Extol him, all people."* (117:1)

> *"All the ends of the earth have seen the salvation of our God."* (98:1)

The exact phrase *all nations* (πάντα τὰ ἔθνη) appears 11 times in the Septuagint's (LXX) translation of the Psalms.[12]

---

[12] I searched this phrase in the Septuagint using Logos Bible

Turning our focus now to Psalm 96, Christopher Little describes verse three as the "Old Testament Great Commission."[13] Although this Psalm has no title, the LXX ascribes it to David.[14] Like other psalms of this kind, Psalm 96 was composed as a tune to be sung at one of the festivals where God was declared as king of the universe - probably the Festival of Tabernacles.[15] The first verse calls for universal praise to Yahweh: *"Sing to the LORD, all the earth!"* (verse 1b). Then in verse two the command rests upon God's people, *"Tell of his salvation from day to day!"* "Tell" is a second person, plural, imperative. It is a command. In typical Hebrew parallelism, the psalmist goes on to say, *"Declare his glory among the nations, his marvelous works among all the peoples."* Once again we encounter an imperative. Both verbs instruct God's people to verbally take the message of his glory to the world. "Tell" carries the meaning of preach or publish, whereas "Declare" has the sense of announcing, recounting, or reporting what God has done.[16] It has the force of reporting a victory which Yahweh has won elsewhere.[17] Both verbs

---

Software. The Septuagint is the Greek Translation of the Old Testament produced at the Library of Alexandria by 70 Jewish Rabbis in the 4th Century BC.

[13] Christopher Little, "Hebrew Literature." Lecture at Columbia International University, Columbia, SC, March 2016.

[14] Marvin E. Tate, *Psalms 51–100*, vol. 20, Word Biblical Commentary (Dallas: Word, Incorporated, 1998), 510.

[15] Robert G. Bratcher and William David Reyburn, *A Translator's Handbook on the Book of Psalms*, UBS Handbook Series (New York: United Bible Societies, 1991), 832.

[16] R. D. Patterson, "1540 סָפַר," ed. R. Laird Harris, Gleason L. Archer Jr., and Bruce K. Waltke, *Theological Wordbook of the Old Testament* (Chicago: Moody Press, 1999), 632.

correspond to the act of preaching. In fact, the LXX translates "tell" as εὐαγγελίζεσθε, which literally means "to preach the good news." It is the same verb used by Jesus in Luke 4 when he said, *"He has anointed me to proclaim good news to the poor."* It is the same verb used by Luke when he said Jesus went about *"proclaiming the good news of God's Kingdom"* (Luke 8:1).

The substance of this proclamation is "glory." In this context *his glory* can be translated "his fame" or "his greatness." All three describe Yahweh as a God who manifests himself (*glory*) by means of his mighty deeds on behalf of his people.[18] And Yahweh's glory is the manifestation of his presence (Numbers 16:19, 32; Ps 102:16, Isa 8:7; 40:5; 60:1–2; cf. Exod. 16:10; 24:16–17; 40:34).[19] But the parallelism of "his marvelous works" in 3b gives strength to the argument that God's people were called to share the news of the creation, the exodus, and other events that detail God's powerful action in the world. Today, God's people should understand this message to be the death, burial, and resurrection of Christ unto repentance for the forgiveness of sin (Corinthians 15:3).[20]

The scope of the command is again the nations. The LXX translates the Hebrew word with the same basic noun used in the Great Commission, ἔθνεσιν.[21] As Ralph Winter has so famously taught us, *ethne* refers to the

---

[17] Marvin E. Tate, *Psalms 51–100*, vol. 20, Word Biblical Commentary (Dallas: Word, Incorporated, 1998), 512.

[18] Bratcher and Reyburn, *A Translator's Handbook on the Book of Psalms*, 833.

[19] Tate, *Psalms 51–100*, 512.

[20] J. I. Packer, "Introduction," in *Psalms*, Crossway Classic Commentaries (Wheaton, IL: Crossway Books, 1993), 46.

[21] *Septuaginta: With Morphology*, electronic ed. (Stuttgart: Deutsche Bibelgesellschaft, 1979), Ps 95:3–6.

smallest division of ethno-linguistic people that the gospel can spread through unhindered. Indeed, no corner of the earth is beyond the reach of this command.

Therefore, this Psalm captures the essence of the Great Commission. God's people are commanded to preach the good news of God's amazing deeds to all nations! The news of God's saving work should be spread abroad day after day until all people and nations know about his glory. This sounds a lot like the Great Commission to me.

Once again we see that the Great Commission of Matthew 28 was not novel. God has been speaking it from the beginning. And he is still speaking his mission to his people in hopes that we will come together under his leadership to take the gospel to the ends of the earth. Let it be   so.

4 JONAH

Jonah is a familiar story. God told the prophet to preach repentance to Nineveh, but he refused. Instead, he sailed in the opposite direction and soon found himself swallowed by a fish and carried back on course. But do we understand the real meaning of this book?

Most of our exposure to Jonah has come from children's picture books. At the same time, many popular speakers tell us that Jonah ended up in the belly of a fish because of disobedience or a failure of faith. Other academics link his reluctance – in light of God's inevitable mercy – to the prophet's unwillingness to be proved a false prophet, since he had previously predicated their destruction.[22] However, the best reading of Jonah's foot-dragging is related to his sour attitude toward the nation and unwillingness to see the blessing of Abraham extended this nation. As Kaiser said, "The text was written ... to encourage the adoption of Yahweh's heart for the nations."[23] Indeed Ezekiel 18:23 did not just apply to the

---

[22] Stephen B. Chapman and Laceye C. Warner, "Evangelism and the Old Testament," *Journal of Theological Interpretation* 2.1 (2008): 43-69.

Jews: "*Do I take any pleasure in the death of the wicked? Declares the Sovereign Lord.*" The clear answer is that He does not.

In this chapter we will see that God sent Jonah to preach repentance to the Ninevites in light of His promise in Genesis 12:3 and under the mandate of Psalm 96:3. God's specific sending of Jonah, and his rebuke of the prophet, reveal much about Yahweh's heart in relation to the missional commands he has given us.

The events in this book took place sometime during the reign of Jeroboam (793–753 BC), the most powerful king of the Northern Kingdom of Israel (2 King 14:25).[24] Before Jeroboam's reign God used the Syrians to torment Israel as a punishment for their sins (cf. 2 Kgs 13:1–3).[25] But political discourse at that time asserted that God would destroy the Ninevites and expand Israel's borders. This was the national hope.[26]

Jonah's story can be outlined in the following way: (1) The prophet received a command from God to go to Nineveh and announce the destruction of that city because of its sins. (2) Jonah rebels against this call and runs in the opposite direction. (3) God retrieves him through the fish and puts him back on mission. (4) Jonah preaches in Nineveh and its people repent. (5) The prophet complains to God that he is too compassionate toward the nations. (6) God rebukes Jonah for attitude.[27]

In the second verse of chapter one Jonah is told,

---

[23] Walter Kaiser, *Mission in the Old Testament* (Grand Rapids: Baker Academic, 2012), 69.

[24] John D. Hannah, "Jonah," in *The Bible Knowledge Commentary: An Exposition of the Scriptures*, 1460–1461.

[25] Billy K. Smith and Franklin S. Page, *Amos, Obadiah, Jonah*, vol. 19B, The New American Commentary (Nashville: Broadman & Holman Publishers, 1995), 204.

[26] Ibid, 203–204.

[27] Ibid.

"Arise, go." The LXX translates this Hebrew word for "go" as πορεύθητι. It is given in the imperative and indeed means to "go" or "travel."[28] It is the same verb – and verb form – used by the resurrected Christ in the Great Commission when He said, "Go into all the world." This is a clear Old Testament example of one of God's people being sent to the nations to preach repentance unto the forgiveness of sins. And much like Hosea and Ezekiel, Jonah was playing a representative role for the people of God.[29]

Jonah was not told to go just anywhere. He was told to go to Israel's chief nemesis among the gentiles. Nineveh was one of the largest and most grand cities of ancient near east. The city was located east of the Tigris near modern Mosul. It had access to water and rich agricultural land. God identifies Nineveh as "that great city."[30] Jonah 3:3 says it took three days to walk across it. Scripture tells us that the city had some 120,000 children, 1,500 towers, and walls rising 200 feet high. Nineveh was truly unique among the known world.[31] God wants us to understand Nineveh as representative of the lost gentile world, much like Rome and Babylon are to be understood in later prophetic writings. God was not just communicating his intentions toward the Ninevites; he was communicating

---

[28] Gerhard Kittel, Gerhard Friedrich, and Geoffrey William Bromiley, *Theological Dictionary of the New Testament* (Grand Rapids, MI: W.B. Eerdmans, 1985), 915.

[29] Ryan D Estelle, *Salvation Through Judgment and Mercy: The Gospel According to Jonah* (New Jersey: PR Publishing, 2005), 33.

[30] Jamieson, Fausset, and Brown, *Commentary Critical and Explanatory on the Whole Bible*, vol. 1, 683. In the Assyria histories of Diodorus Diculus, Nineveh is identified as four hundred eighty stadia in circumference, one hundred fifty stadia in length, and ninety stadia in breadth, as taken by Arbaces the Mede, in the reign of Sardanapalus, about the seventh year of Uzziah.

[31] Kaiser, *Mission in the Old Testament*, 70.

his purposes for all the nations.

After the fish spits Jonah up, God reiterates his command telling him to *"Arise, go to Nineveh"* (3:2); but this time He includes *"and proclaim to it **the message I tell you"*** (3:3). This is different than the first call in 1:2 where Jonah was told to *"cry against it; for their wickedness has come up to me."* The LXX translates the world "proclaim" as κήρυξον and message as κήρυγμα (*kerygma*) – both forms of a powerful word the writers of the New Testament would later use to describe the content of the gospel and the action of presenting it (Rom 16:25; 1 Cor. 1:21; 15:14, Titus 1:3).[32] Indeed, *kerygma* would become the technical term for the life, death, burial, resurrection, and return of Jesus.

Jonah then walks 900 miles under this divine compulsion across desert routes to declare, *"Yet forty days, and Nineveh shall be overthrown!"* We read this in the English and view "overthrown" as an immutable divine decree of destruction. However, as the Jewish expositor Rashi explains, "The word 'overthrown' has two senses, good and bad. If they do not repent they will be 'destroyed.' But if they repent they shall indeed be 'overthrown,' for they will have changed from evil to good."[33] Indeed, this word is translated to "overthrown" a mere 13 times in the Old Testament but is translated as "turn" 576 times.[34]

Amazingly, the people "believed" (3:5) and turned. One does not need a hyper imagination to hear Peter saying at Pentecost, *"You killed the Messiah! Repent!"* Indeed, at Jonah's call the people of Nineveh obeyed the first command of Jesus, *"Repent and believe in the gospel"* (Mark 1:15). The message, the linguistics, the actions, and the

---

[32] Rosemary Nixon, "The Message of Jonah." *The Bible Speaks Today* (England, Intervarsity Press, 2011), 163.

[33] Ibid., 165.

[34] I used the Logos Bible Study Software world study tool to calculate this.

scope are all connected to the mission Jesus left his disciples – the mission of God. But we cannot depart this book until we grasp the lesson God taught Jonah in chapter four.

When Nineveh repented God relented of the disaster Jonah prophesied. Jonah was very angry about this (4:1). This is odd to our ears because today we pray for the mass repentance of entire cities and rejoice at a single convert. But Jonah would have none of it. In verse 4:2 one can almost hear Jonah yelling at God, "I knew you were going to forgive them – you loving God! That is why I didn't want to go to Ninevah!" In this prayer, Jonah reveals the source of his disobedience. He wanted God to destroy them!

Jonah then politely asks God to take his life. Not hearing a response, he wanders outside the city, builds a shelter and falls asleep. God then caused a plant to grow over Jonah that provided shade, and Jonah was glad. But the next morning God appointed a worm to attack the plant and it withered. As the sun rose high, God brought an east wind to scorch the exposed prophet. Jonah informs God of his desire for death. Let us recount the dialog that ensues:

> *But God said to Jonah, "Do you do well to be angry for the plant?" And he said, "Yes, I do well to be angry, angry enough to die."[10] And the Lord said, "You pity the plant, for which you did not labor, nor did you make it grow, which came into being in a night and perished in a night.[11] And should not I pity Nineveh, that great city, in which there are more than 120,000 persons who do not know their right hand from their left, and also much cattle?"[35]*

God implies that Jonah was more concerned about the plant which perished overnight than about the people of

---

[35] *The Holy Bible: English Standard Version* (Wheaton: Standard Bible Society, 2001), Jon 4:8–11.

Nineveh. Jonah was prepared to die for a plant but was unwilling to live for 600,000 people created in God's image. God then challenges the prophet's attitude with a poignant question: *"And should not I pity Nineveh?"* The answer was clear. God cared deeply for all the nations. This passion had already been echoed throughout the law and the prophets. Jonah apparently missed it. Or worse, he had grown completely indifferent to the fate of those outside Israel.[36] Jonah was guilty of the Great Omission in light of the Great Commission, so to speak, of Psalms 96:3. As God's representative, he no longer carried the vision given to Abraham of blessing all the families of the earth.

Many Christians today (myself included at times), have understood the Great Commission but stood apathetically aside. Some have heard the call to go to Nineveh (or Bagdad, or Tehran, or Mecca) and have thrown themselves into a new job or a new ministry or a new "calling." For all practical purposes, we have sailed to Tarshish.

Jonah reminds us that the Great Commission is God's mission. It is His passion. And he will bring it to completion. If we, like Israel of Jonah's day, fail to "go" and "proclaim" the message of God's glory, God will dynamically arrange history to move either the nations to the church or the church to the nations.[37]

---

[36] Smith and Page, *Amos, Obadiah, Jonah*, 282.

[37] See Ralph Winter, "The Kingdom Strikes Back: Ten Epochs of Redemptive History," *Perspectives on the World Christian Movement: A Reader*, ed. Ralph Winter and Stephen Hawthrone (Pasadena: William Carey Library, 2011), 209-227.

5 COMMISSIONS OF CHRIST

The book began by saying the Great Commission of Matthew 28:18-20 contains the mission of the church. Although this position can be argued, I will not here come to its defense. Sufficient scholarship has established Matthew 28 as a seminal articulation of the mission of God.[38] So far I have shown how this Great Commission is rooted in the commissions given to God's patriarchs, people, and prophets in Genesis, Psalms, and Jonah respectively. Jesus was not teaching something new. Furthermore, Matthew 28 is not the only place Jesus gives his disciples God's mission. A survey of the New Testament reveals five distinct commissions of the resurrected Christ. To understand these allow me to first establish some context.

Christ was sent from God to preach the gospel from town-to-town: *"And he said to them, 'Let us go on to the next towns, that I may preach there also, for that is why I came out'"* (Mark 1:38). Again we see the Greek word κηρύσσω used

---

[38] See Tokyo 2010 Declaration (p. 2); William Carey, *An Enquiry Into the Obligation of Christians to Use Means for the Conversion of the Heathens*; Steven Hawthorne, "Mandate of the Mountain"; Arthur Glasser, preface to *The Mission of the Church in the World* by Roger Hedlund, etc.

for preach. Jesus was sent (the idea of *going* out from someone) to preach. The basic context of the preaching is given in Mark 1:15: "*The time is fulfilled, and the kingdom of God is at hand; repent and believe the gospel*" (cf. Matthew 4:17). This was Jesus' message. It was the same message that John the Baptist preached (Matthew 3:2) and it contained the promise of forgiveness of sins (Luke 3:3). Notice this is the same message that Jonah preached with the same verbs. It is the same verbs used by the Psalmist and the same action of leaving – for the sake of the nations – as Adam and Abram. Jesus came to carry forward the already established mission of God.

We must here pause to say, that although Jesus did come to carry on the mission, he also had a unique role to play. Jesus came not only as the model missionary but as the Lamb of God; the only one who can and would die an atoning death for the sins of the world. He did this once and for all, and there is no need for a continuing sacrifice (1 Peter 3:18).

Nevertheless, he also came to train men in his missionary ways. Jesus first modeled missionary activity (Matthew 4:19). After they watched Jesus preach the gospel of the kingdom it was their turn. He told them to "go" and "*proclaim as you go, the kingdom of heaven is at hand*" (Matthew 10:8). Although they were told to stay in Israel at first, the scope of this mission was world-wide.[39]

After this "*the Lord appointed seventy-two others and sent them on ahead of him, two by two, into every town and place he himself was about to go*" (Luke 10:1)." Here we see that Jesus was expanding his missional training program. The apostles were not the only "sent ones." Jesus here expands the ministry beyond the Twelve and those original witnesses to the resurrection.[40] In fact, Jesus told this same group to

---

[39] Leon Morris, *The Gospel According to Matthew*, The Pillar New Testament Commentary (Grand Rapids, MI; Leicester, England: W.B. Eerdmans; Inter-Varsity Press, 1992), 245.

pray for more laborers: *"The harvest is plentiful, but the laborers are few. Therefore, pray earnestly to the Lord of the harvest to send out laborers into his harvest"* (Luke 10:2). Interestingly, the word here used for "sent" is ἐκβάλλω. It is the same word used elsewhere to cast out a demon. It is also the same Greek word in the LXX used to translate the "Go" of Abram's commission in Genesis 12:1. Might God have anticipated the unwillingness of his people to go and thus used an appropriate verb (reference Jonah)? Whatever the case, the big point is that Jesus was expanding their understanding and making clear that his mission has a world-wide scope.

Immediately after the resurrection, Jesus gave his disciples a curious instruction. First, the angels told Mary Magdalene and the other Mary to tell the disciples, *"He is going before you to Galilee."* As the women departed they ran into Jesus. The first words the resurrected Christ spoke where these: *"Greetings! Do not be afraid; go and tell my brothers to go to Galilee, and there they will see me"* (Matthew 28:10). It is fascinating Jesus told his disciples to walk 70 miles to hear from him again. Was he building suspense?

Many Missiologists understand Jesus to be setting up the Great Commission in some way. Dr. Little suggests that Jesus wanted them to go to Galilee because the region was the gateway to the nations (*Galilee of the Gentiles*, Matthew 4:15).[41] Others see Jesus taking them to the location of the other commissions. Or perhaps he just wanted a location he knew would accommodate a large crowd. As Leon Morris said, "It is possible that *his disciples* here means his followers as a whole. Jesus appeared to small numbers in Jerusalem, but Paul speaks of an

---

[40] Darrell L. Bock, *Luke: 9:51–24:53*, vol. 2, Baker Exegetical Commentary on the New Testament (Grand Rapids, MI: Baker Academic, 1996), 994.

[41] Little, Lecture at Columbia International University, Columbia, SC, March 2016."

appearance to more than 500 people (1 Cor. 15:6), and this may well have been in Galilee."[42] If Morris' hunch is correct, Jesus here intended to launch all his followers to the nations to make disciples.[43]

THE COMMISSION OF LUKE 24

The resurrected Christ first appeared to his 11 remaining disciples as they were gathered in the upper room the Sunday after His crucifixion.[44] Jesus said to them:

> *"Thus it is written, that the Christ should suffer and on the third day rise from the dead,[47] and that repentance and forgiveness of sins should be proclaimed in his name to all nations, beginning from Jerusalem.[48] You are witnesses of these things.[49] And behold, I am sending the promise of my Father upon you.* (Luke 24:46-49)

Although the verb *proclaimed* in this passage is recorded in the passive voice, it has the force of a command.[45] Nevertheless, the risen Christ says that the same message Jonah carried (repentance for forgiveness) will be delivered in the same way (proclaimed), to the same people (gentiles). To substantiate this mission was nothing new, Jesus prefaces his instruction with "Thus it is written." He

---

[42] Morris, *The Gospel According to Matthew.*

[43] Robert Coleman shares Morris' view as well, but there are others such as John Harvey who limit this commission to the 12.

[44] Joel B. Green, *The Gospel of Luke,* The New International Commentary on the New Testament (Grand Rapids, MI: W.B. Eerdmans Publishing Company, 1997), 852.

[45] John Harvey, "Mission in Jesus' Teaching," *Mission in the New Testament: An Evangelical Approach,* ed. by William Larkin and Joel Williams (Mayknoll, New York: Orbis Books, 1999), 47.

was referencing the scriptures they had at the time – the Old Testament. Christ is commenting on the mission previously articulated in the Law and the Prophets."[46] Did he mean to reference Adam, Noah, Abram, Isaac, Jacob, Psalm 96, and Jonah? Or was he referencing other scriptures yet to be highlighted? Whatever the case, Jesus was shining light on something very old, rather than creating something new.

THE COMMISSION OF JOHN 20

It was likely during this same visit to the upper room that Jesus gave what is known as the Johannine Commission: *"Peace be upon you. As the Father has sent me, even so I am sending you"* (John 20:21). The idea of being sent is the overriding motif in John's gospel. There are 39 verses related to *sending*, the vast majority of which the Father is sending the Son.[47] Köstenberger's commentary on this passage is worth quoting at length:

---

[46] I. Howard Marshall, *The Gospel of Luke: A Commentary on the Greek Text*, New International Greek Testament Commentary (Exeter: Paternoster Press, 1978), 905.

[47] Christopher Little, Classroom Lecture, Columbia International University, April 2016: 3:34, 4:34, 5:23-24, 5:30, 5:36-38; 6:29, 6:38, 6:44, 6:57, 7:16-18, 7:28-33, 8:16-29, 8:42, 9:4, 10:36, 11:42, 12:44-45, 12:49, 13:16, 13:20, 14:24, 15:21, 16:5, 17:3, 17:8; 17:18, 17:21, 17:23, 17:25, 20:21.

The focus of the present unit is Jesus' commissioning statement "As the Father has sent me, so I am sending you" (cf. Matt. 28:18–20; Luke 24:46–49), which climaxes in the characterization of Jesus as the sent Son. The disciples are drawn into the unity and mission of Father and Son. Succession is important both in the OT and in Second Temple literature. In the present Gospel, Jesus succeeds the Baptist and is followed by both the Spirit and the Twelve (minus Judas), who serve as representatives of the new messianic community. OT narratives involving succession feature Joshua (following Moses) and Elisha (succeeding Elijah).[48]

In this section Köstenberger validates the idea we began with in this section. Jesus was sent by the Father to preach repentance and belief for the forgiveness of sin. Now he is passing the baton to his followers – "representatives of the new messianic community." All those who confess Jesus as Lord are part of this community and share in this responsibility.

THE COMMISSION IN MARK

A plain reading of the Mark 16:14 places this commission in the upper room as well.[49] However, because of its questionable authenticity and similarity with Matthew's commission, many scholars view Mark 16:14-18 as Peter's version of the Great Commission in Galilee. But perhaps, Marvin Newell has it right. In his book *Commissioned* he argues that Mark's commission was given in the upper room 8 days after the resurrection. Whatever the case, the command is clear:

---

[48] Andreas J. Köstenberger, *John*, Baker Exegetical Commentary on the New Testament (Grand Rapids, MI: Baker Academic, 2004), 573–574.

[49] John D. Grassmick, "Mark," in *The Bible Knowledge Commentary: An Exposition of the Scriptures*, 195.

> *"Go into all the world and proclaim the gospel to the whole creation.[16] Whoever believes and is baptized will be saved, but whoever does not believe will be condemned.[17] And these signs will accompany those who believe: in my name they will cast out demons; they will speak in new tongues;[18] they will pick up serpents with their hands; and if they drink any deadly poison, it will not hurt them; they will lay their hands on the sick, and they will recover."* (Mark 16:15-18)

The reader should not miss that the commands (imperatives) to go (πορεύομαι) and preach (κηρύσσω) the gospel (εὐαγγέλιον) are the same Greek words we have seen emerge in the LXX throughout our study. Moreover, we also see in this commission a world-wide scope that encompasses both land (all the world) and people (the whole creation) just like the commission given to Abram (country and kindred). Also notice that, like Abram, obedience to the command comes with a promise. Here we see the promise of signs and power. In John we saw the promise of peace. In Matthew it was the assurance that He will be with us always.

THE COMMISSION OF MATTHEW 28

The upper room appearances (whenever they were) likely gave the disciples the faith they needed to make the trip to Galilee (isn't it strange they hadn't yet departed?). Although we have already looked at Matthew 28 in some detail, there is still more. First, the imperative in Matthew's

[50] R. T. France, *The Gospel of Matthew*, The New International Commentary on the New Testament (Grand Rapids, MI: Eerdmans Publishing Co. 2007), 1115.

[51] Although I am sure this construction is not original, I do not know any anyone else making the differentiation.

version of the commission is "make disciples." Note that the command in this verse is not to proclaim the good news.[50] Rather *making disciples* is the primary means (task) and the end state is that people of all nations will one day worship before God's throne (Revelation 7:9).[51] Preaching the gospel is the initial step to making disciples; and it is wrapped into and implied within the task of disciple making. Jesus did not need to include the command "preach" in Matthew's commission. Preaching is the first necessary step of disciple making after "going."

In the next part of the verse Jesus tells how we should carry out this task of making disciples – "baptizing" and "teaching them to obey everything I have commanded." Since teaching disciples to obey Jesus' commands includes this very command (the Great Commission), our mission includes making disciples who teach their disciples to obey the command to make disciples.[52] This is the heart of God's mission; and it makes sense of the promise of multiplication given to Abram. We are commanded to multiply spiritual generations to all nations through disciple making.

THE COMMISSION OF ACTS

The final commission of the resurrected Christ is recorded in Acts chapter 1 and is given right before Jesus ascends into heaven.[53] The location was the Mount of Olives (v. 12). He said: "But you will receive power when the Holy Spirit has come upon you, and you will be my witnesses in Jerusalem and in all Judea and Samaria, and to the end of the earth" (Acts 1:8). As Newman and Nida

---

[52] See Robert Coleman, *The Master Plan of Evangelism* (Grand Rapid, MI: Revell, 2006).

[53] John B. Polhill, *Acts*, vol. 26, The New American Commentary (Nashville: Broadman & Holman Publishers, 1992), 84.

said in the USB Handbook:

> *You will be witnesses* for me is not simply a statement of future fact, **but it is given in the nature of a command.** The Greek term usually translated as "witness" is found thirteen times in Acts, and the basic meaning is "one who testifies." Only in 22:20 can it possibly be stretched to mean "martyr," and even in that context the primary meaning is that of "one who gives testimony."[54]

Jesus commands his disciple to be his witness – to proclaim the kerygma – to the end of the earth. The emphasis in this passage is on the scope of the mission. The disciples were certainly called to make disciples by proclaiming repentance unto the forgiveness of sin in Jerusalem. Peter did this marvelously on the day of Pentecost. However, it seems crystal-clear from this passage that they were not supposed to stop there. They were mandated to witness to the gospel in ever expanding regions until all nations were under the Lordship of the King.

---

[54] Barclay Moon Newman and Eugene Albert Nida, *A Handbook on the Acts of the Apostles*, UBS Handbook Series (New York: United Bible Societies, 1972), 18.

6 SO WHAT?

In this book I pointed out, through an explanation of several Old Testament and New Testament passages, that the mission of the church is go and make disciples of all nations by preaching repentance and belief for the forgiveness of sin, baptizing, and teaching them to obey all that Jesus has commanded – even (and especially) this command. I have demonstrated that this command did not originate with Jesus. Rather it has antecedents from Genesis to Jonah and beyond. At this point you may ask "So what?" Allow me to leave you with five take-aways:

1. *It is God's Mission and his people are slow to obey.* Although Adam and Noah were explicitly commanded to fill the earth, their descendants gathered at Babel. Although Abram obeyed the command to go, the generations after him lost sight of both the command and the promise. Although David reiterated the command to "go" in the Psalms, a few hundred years later Jonah refused. Although Jesus told his disciples to go and preach and make disciples of all nations, it was God who was the primary mover in the book of Acts. God initiated Pentecost. God allowed the persecution that scattered the

apostles (7:54-8:8). God told Philip to *"Rise and go toward the south"* (9:26). God encountered Saul on the road to Damascus. God gave Cornelius a vision (10:3). God put Peter into a trance (10:10). God initiated the gentile Pentecost (10:44). God set apart Paul and Barnabas for the work of ministry (13:2). Indeed, it seems like no one goes on mission in the book of Acts – or the Bible – without God's dramatic empowering or prodding.

What ought we to conclude from this? The Great Commission is indeed God's mission. He will bring it to pass. Those who are willing to be sacrificially obedient will be blessed. Not with riches, but with God. Abraham is the person in our survey that was the most obedient. And he has a corresponding place in our faith.

2.   *As a church we are mostly walking in the faith blessing of Abraham, but not his blessings of multiplication.* The faith blessing is awesome and indeed critical.But we must remember that it is not ours to keep. The blessing is for the world. Most of us are not yet walking in Abraham's blessing of multiplication (Hebrew 6:14). As ministers of the word (Acts 6:4) we must hold the mission – the commands – and all its associated blessings before the church. Will you?

3.   *The missional commands of Jesus are very narrow.* They are "go," "proclaim/preach/declare," and "make disciples." That's it. These are the tasks of the mission. Wherever *justice*, *peace*, the *environment*, etc. replace these tasks – and makes them an end in themselves – biblical mission no longer exists.

4.   *The scope of the mission is universal.* Every single passage we reviewed defined the scope of the mission as the whole world – all the nations. While it is true that we are part of that world wherever we are (Acts 1:8), we must fight the ever-present danger of ethnocentrism. Preachers of God's word must continue to proclaim God's heart for every tribe and language and people and nation (Rev 5:9). Teachers of God's word ought to develop biblical means

to help disciples determine where they should "go." All Christians should honestly ask themselves if what they are doing relates to "all the nations" – either through direct contact, disciple making, teaching, or another supporting task.

5.   *Everyone must relate their Christian service to God's mission.* Building on the idea above, and returning to the idea of synchronizing tasks of purposes introduced in the introduction, church leaders must ask themselves, "How does the mission of my church relate to the mission of *the* church? There will be some churches in Iran who are doing direct missional work among the nations. These direct-missional churches also exist in New York, Los Angeles, Deerborn, and many other places. There are other churches who do not have any direct cross-cultural work but are empowering those who do thorough giving, teaching, prayer and other essential tasks. These churches are still part of the mission.

There are other churches that focus all their efforts on helping to alleviate suffering among the unreached. If this task is directly related to helping another church or mission agency make disciples, then they too are part of God's mission. God is using them in a supporting role to bring about an end state that is the church's task – to make disciples of all nations. This is indeed how military missions are organized. The main subordinate effort keeps the task and purpose of its parent unit (in this case, *make disciple of all nations so that all people will worship God at the end of the age.* But sister units take on alternative *tasks* with the *purpose* of assisting the main effort to accomplish their task (make disciples).

Therefore, leaders in the Christian community ought to help those people and churches who are called to a task other than *make disciple of all nations* see how their calling fits into the larger mission of the church. If a local leader cannot directly relate his mission to the greater mission of the church – he has ceased to be on mission. But the solution to this problem is not disassociation – it is more discipleship. Classes on the Mission of God ought to be part of the required curriculum of every bible college and seminary. Elder boards and parish councils ought to ensure their mission is synchronized with God's. Churches ought to preach about the Mission of God before they preach their local vision. One-on-one disciple makers ought to prioritize helping their mentee relate his/her life work to the Great Commission. Fathers ought to cast vision of God's great plan around the dinner table. Denomination leaders ought use the Mission of God as a source ecumenical unity at home and increased collaboration on the mission field. Writers and creators – much better than me – ought to find ways to capture the attention of the an increasingly larger portion of the church with these truths.

Now it's your turn. Get the Great Commission firmly established in your heart. Prayerful, find where your calling, gifts, passion, and influence intersect with the Mission of God and get after it – for his glory among the nations.

Joshua Gilliam holds an MA in Muslim studies from Columbia International University and an MDiv from Beacon University. A 2000 graduate of West Point, Josh served multiple deployments in Iraq and Afghanistan as both an infantryman and a chaplain. Josh now leads COLTTI, a company established in 2016 with the sole purpose of funding the Great Commission among unengaged people groups. All profit generated by COLETTI – including this book – go toward *the mission of God.*

Lean more at www.coletticoffee.com

www.ingramcontent.com/pod-product-compliance
Lightning Source LLC
Chambersburg PA
CBHW031247130726
47988CB00008B/3276